SPEAK UP!
CONFRONTING DISCRIMINATION IN YOUR DAILY LIFE™

CONFRONTING
ANTI-SEMITISM

KRISTINA LYN HEITKAMP

Rosen
YA™
New York

Published in 2018 by The Rosen Publishing Group, Inc.
29 East 21st Street, New York, NY 10010

Copyright © 2018 by The Rosen Publishing Group, Inc.

First Edition

Library of Congress Cataloging-in-Publication Data

Names: Heitkamp, Kristina Lyn, author.
Title: Confronting anti-Semitism / Kristina Lyn Heitkamp.
Description: New York: Rosen Publishing, 2018 | Series: Speak up! confronting discrimination in your daily life | Includes bibliographical references and index. | Audience: Grades 7–12.
Identifiers: LCCN 2017016943| ISBN 9781508177425 (library bound) | ISBN 9781508177432 (pbk.) | ISBN 9781508177449 (6 pack)
Subjects: LCSH: Antisemitism—Juvenile literature. | Antisem-itism—United States—Juvenile literature. | Religious tolerance—Juvenile literature.
Classification: LCC DS145 .H4243 2017 | DDC 305.892/4—dc23
LC record available at https://lccn.loc.gov/2017016943

Manufactured in China

CONTENTS

INTRODUCTION   4

CHAPTER ONE
EMBRACE DIVERSITY, END DISCRIMINATION   8

CHAPTER TWO
REMEMBER, REFLECT, AND COMMIT TO CHANGE   16

CHAPTER THREE
RECOGNIZING CONTEMPORARY ANTI-SEMITISM   25

CHAPTER FOUR
HEAR SOMETHING, SAY SOMETHING   32

CHAPTER FIVE
NO JUSTIFICATION FOR DISCRIMINATION   40

CHAPTER SIX
STAY CALM AND CARRY ON   48

GLOSSARY   54
FOR MORE INFORMATION   56
FOR FURTHER READING   59
BIBLIOGRAPHY   60
INDEX   62

INTRODUCTION

O n a cold December night in 1993, someone snuck into the Schnitzers' yard and hurled a cinder block through the window of five-year-old Isaac's bedroom. The window had been decorated with Star of David decals and a menorah—a symbol used to honor the Jewish holiday of Hanukkah. The heavy cement brick landed on Isaac's bed, but he was fortunately watching TV with his younger sister in the family room.

This incident was the tipping point of discrimination that had invaded Billings, Montana. Anti-Semitism and racism had escalated in the capital city. Hate-spewing fliers had been circulated, hidden in newspapers and shoved under windshield wipers. A Jewish cemetery was desecrated and graves were overturned. The local synagogue received bomb threats. Other minorities were also targeted. An African Methodist Episcopal Church faced harassment and intimidation from a group of skinheads and Ku Klux Klan members. Racist graffiti appeared on a wall near the church. A Native American home was also vandalized with a swastika and crude words.

Then the hate turned violent. First with a beer bottle thrown into the home of a Jewish family, and then the attack on the Schnitzers' home. The community was on edge, wondering when and where the next assault would happen. Tammie Schnitzer shared her story with the press and urged synagogue members to speak out.

Unfortunately, Billings, Montana, is not the only community in the United States to have been devastated by hate crimes. In February 2017, more than one hundred Jewish tombstones were vandalized in the Mount Carmel Cemetery in Philadelphia, Pennsylvania.

Several faith leaders in the community also wanted to join the fight against hate. The citizens of Billings banded together.

Hundreds of menorahs appeared in windows of Christian homes. Regardless of their faith, many residents attended services at the African Methodist Episcopal Church until the skinheads stopped harassing the congregation. Volunteers from a local painters' union

A nine-candle menorah is used during the Jewish holiday of Hanukkah. It was a menorah such as this one that glowed in the Schnitzers' window in Billings, Montana, when their window was smashed in an anti-Semitic attack.

painted over the graffiti on the Native American house. The local paper, the *Billings Gazette,* printed a full-page menorah and asked citizens to display it in their windows as a symbol of their collective dedication to the principle of religious liberty embodied in the US constitution.

The haters lashed out. More homes and a Methodist church were vandalized. Car windows with menorah symbols were smashed. Shots were fired into a Catholic school that had also joined the resistance against discrimination. But Billings residents rose above the hate. Soon, nearly 10,000 windows proudly displayed a menorah in an act of solidarity. The story has inspired and encouraged other communities around the United States to reject hate crimes.

But it takes more than a public display to battle anti-Semitism. It is a day-to-day effort to recognize, confront, and report the behavior. It is acknowledging that hateful acts are not normal and not the way to treat one another. Anti-Semitism continues around the world. Discrimination, in general, has evolved to include online messaging and cyberbullying. In the face of modern anti-Semitism, many are unsure how to respond. Some may opt to remain silent, while others may feel immobilized. But by not standing up and confronting the discrimination, the cycle of hate continues.

CHAPTER ONE

EMBRACE DIVERSITY, END DISCRIMINATION

A ccording to the annual Hate Crimes Statistics Report gathered by Federal Bureau of Investigation (FBI), there were almost 6,000 hate crime incidents in 2015. Of those crimes, nearly 20 percent of the victims were targeted because of religious discrimination. A "hate crime" is defined as a "traditional offense, such as vandalism or violence, but with an added element of bias or discrimination."

WHAT IS DISCRIMINATION?

Plainly put, the word "discrimination" is defined as "singling out or distinguishing one thing from another." People use discrimination to make decisions every day, such as choosing chocolate ice cream over vanilla. But in the context of human rights, "discrimination" is defined as "unjust or unequal treatment of a person based on specific characteristics, such as race, religion or sex." Other illegal forms of discrimination include ableism, classism, and biases against immigrant and LGBTQ+ communities.

Not all forms of unequal treatment are illegal. The justice system recognizes both unlawful and lawful discrimination. For example, if a customer walks into a coffee shop barefoot and without a shirt, the owner can refuse to serve him. A sign next to the door might read: No shoes, no shirt, no service. This is lawful discrimination. But if the same customer were to return with shoes and a shirt, and the owner still refused service based on the color of his skin or because he was wearing a Star of David necklace, that would qualify as unlawful discrimination. Federal and state laws prohibit unlawful discrimination, but it can happen almost anywhere, including businesses, schools, or places of employment.

During World War II, the Nazi occupation of Paris affected everyone, including young people. This leisure park displayed a sign that declared the area reserved for children but forbidden to Jews.

Discrimination is often founded in a misconception or on a stereotype. A stereotype is an oversimplified generalization about a person or group of people. For example, the belief that all Jews are cheap or all Muslims are terrorists. Stereotypes can begin with a preconceived notion based on false ideas that evolves into a person's ideology, such as anti-Semitism.

OPINIONS AND CONVICTION

An "ideology" is "a collection of ideas and beliefs that construct and guide a person's behavior and perception of the world." Ideological views are usually formed with influence from family, school, or friends. Ideologies can be religious, political, or ethical. A person can hold several different ideologies that motivate them to action or inaction. Radicalism, conservatism, and liberalism are all political ideologies.

An anti-Semitic ideology is a collection of negative opinions and hostile attitudes toward the Jewish community with a moral value justifying the discrimination. The manifestation of an anti-Semitic ideology may be based on false truths or myths and then justified based on the person's current reality. For example, if an anti-Semite believes that Jews control all financial power, it is possible that this person may feel powerless over his or her own life or feel that Jews have caused him or her to be poor.

RELIGIOUS DISCRIMINATION

Religious discrimination occurs when a person is treated unfavorably because of their religion or religious beliefs. It is illegal to harass or discriminate against a person based on their religion. US law protects people belonging to traditional and organized religions, such as Judaism, Buddhism, Islam, or Christianity. The law also protects religious minorities who genuinely practice their own ethical or moral beliefs.

An employer cannot discriminate against or segregate an employee based on religion, including religious attire. In 2010, nineteen-year-old Muslim employee Umme-Hani Khan was fired from the clothing store Abercrombie & Fitch

During a 2011 press conference in San Francisco, former Abercrombie & Fitch employee Umme-Hani Khan wears a purple hijab as she describes her discrimination experience.

for wearing her hijab, a religious headscarf. The company first asked Khan to wear headscarves that matched the company's colors. She agreed. A few months later, Khan was informed that her hijab violated the company-wide dress code. Managers told her if she failed to adhere to the prescribed dress code, she would be removed from the work schedule. Weeks later, Khan was fired.

A US district judge found Abercrombie liable for religious discrimination. The company paid a settlement fee of $71,000 and changed their policies. The US Equal Employment Opportunity Commission released a statement from Khan after the ruling: "The judge's ruling affirms why I challenged my termination when it happened. It is important for people stand up to discrimination when they experience it, because the law is on our side. I am hopeful that the policy changes will ensure what happened to me never happens to another A&F employee again."

WHAT IS ANTI-SEMITISM?

"Discrimination against Jews" is called "anti-Semitism." In 1879, German agitator Wilhelm Marr popularized the term to help build a political movement to oppress Jews. Sometimes there is confusion on the semantics of the word. The word "Semite" has historically referred to people who speak a Semitic language, such as Arabic, Amharic, Tigrinya, and Hebrew. But the modern definition refers solely to people who are part of the Jewish community. Thus, it would follow that anti-Semitism refers to discrimination against and hostility toward Jews and the Jewish community.

Anti-Semitism can take on different forms, such as stereotyping Jewish people or religious teachings that promote oppression and inferiority of Jews. Some anti-Semitic groups openly publicize their beliefs, such as neo-Nazi organizations, while other anti-Semitic groups refer to their ideology by another name. The Christian Identity is a religious ideology that believes Caucasian people of European descent are superior. Members also consider Jews the satanic offspring of the biblical Eve and the Serpent. The hate group justifies their anti-Semitic violence in the name of Christianity. Another ideology that spouts anti-Semitic and racist rhetoric under a different name is the Alternative Right, or Alt Right. They believe that white identity and white privilege are under siege by political correctness gone mad and other multicultural forces. Members reject traditional conservative views based on the belief that modern conservatives are weak because they do not support anti-Semitism and racism. The Traditional Youth Network (TYN) is another racist and anti-Semitic interpretation of Christianity. The group aims to be a resource for high school and college students. While TYN members claim to support diversity, their definition is exclusive and promotes segregation. Anti-Semitism affects the Jewish community the same way and should be challenged, regardless of the group's name or so-called justification.

Another form of discrimination is anti-Zionism. Zionism is a movement that supports the return of Jewish people to the Holy Land of Israel. It is the foundation of Jewish religion and is included in prayers, rituals, and culture. Modern Zionism emerged after the Holocaust and its horrific genocide of Jews. It combines the traditional historic ties to a homeland with the modern

Israel and the Palestinians

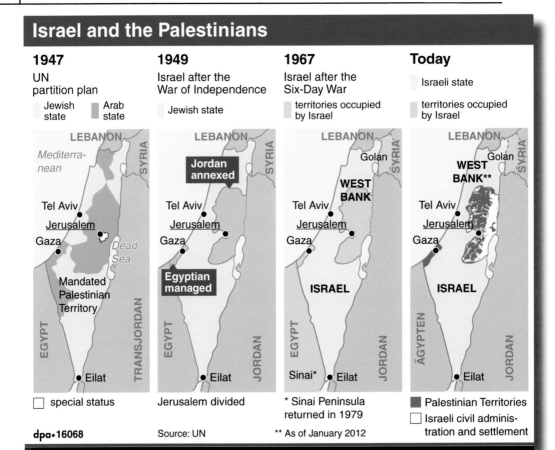

1947
UN partition plan

Jewish state
Arab state

1949
Israel after the War of Independence

Jewish state

1967
Israel after the Six-Day War

territories occupied by Israel

Today

Israeli state

territories occupied by Israel

special status

Jerusalem divided

Source: UN

* Sinai Peninsula returned in 1979

** As of January 2012

Palestinian Territories

Israeli civil adminis- tration and settlement

dpa·16068

These maps illustrate the historic and ongoing struggle between Israelis and Palestinians. The conflict began as a battle over land and has erupted into a religious war, including anti-Zionism.

concept of "nationalism," which is "the ideology of having a shared common origin, ethnicity, and culture." A similar example of nationalism would be that Italians feel Italy is their national homeland. "Anti-Zionism" is "the belief that Jews do not have a right to their own national homeland." It is a form of anti-Semitism disguised under another name.

MYTHS AND FACTS

MYTH
Jews are a race, not a religion.

Fact
This was a cornerstone of Nazi policy, but it is entirely un-scientific to identify the Jewish faith and common culture as a race and not as a religious and cultural heritage.

MYTH
Jews want to take over the world.

Fact
This is a common conspiracy theory that many white supremacist groups have used as a form of control and bullying. In fact, throughout history, Jews have been a minority and are often persecuted.

MYTH
Jews are cheap, greedy, and good with money.

Fact
Jews are like any group of people; some are good with money while others are not.

CHAPTER TWO

REMEMBER, REFLECT, AND COMMIT TO CHANGE

H istorians have referred to anti-Semitism as the oldest hate in history. The prejudice started as a battle over religious beliefs that evolved into a full-blown ideology that systematically discriminated, suppressed, and finally motivated genocide. Some think the hate began and ended during the Nazi era and World War II. But it began long before and continues to thrive today.

OLD HATE

Hebrews, or early Jewish people, faced sporadic discrimination because they were unwilling to assimilate and accept the prominent religion. During the first 1,000 years of Christianity, Catholic leaders indoctrinated a myth that Jews killed Jesus. However, Jewish law forbade crucifixion. Scholars and historians widely agree that Jesus was executed by Roman rulers living in Israel, who crucified thousands of Jews, including others who were killed on the same day as Jesus. But the myth continued.

During the Middle Ages, hatred grew as the Jewish people were depicted not as humans but as monsters. It was rumored that Jews had devil's horns and a tail and performed satanic rituals. "Blood libel" was "a false belief that Jews used the blood of Christian children in religious rituals, including the making of Passover bread, or matzo." The myth reached far and wide. In Syria, nine Jews were accused of murdering a

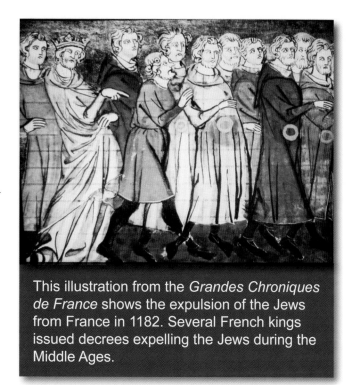

This illustration from the *Grandes Chroniques de France* shows the expulsion of the Jews from France in 1182. Several French kings issued decrees expelling the Jews during the Middle Ages.

friar and his Muslim servant in order to use their blood for Passover. The Jews were convicted, spreading the Damascus blood libel lie as truth. Jews became a target of hate time and time again. During the First Crusade of the eleventh century, Pope Urban II invited Christians of Europe to defend the Holy Land from Muslims and Jews. Invaders of the Jewish communities looted, raped, and murdered. When the bubonic plague swept through Europe killing more than twenty million people, the Jews were blamed (although they were also dying from the disease) and accused of plotting to spread the plague by poisoning wells. It is estimated that 100,000 Jews were killed and burned alive for blood libel, spreading the plague, and other false accusations.

RACE, RELIGION, AND ETHNICITY

Although all humans belong to the same species, *Homo sapiens*, we often want to categorize people in order to better understand them or place them in the world. Race, religion, ethnicity, and culture are some of the tools societies use to differentiate from one another. Though race is a term used to biologically distinguish between different physical appearances, such as skin color, scientists have found the genetic variation between races to be very small and almost insignificant. In a more accurate description, race would be used to distinguish humans from other types of hominids, such as orangutans or chimpanzees. Humans belong to the same race—the human race.

Another identifier is ethnicity. This term is used to describe a person's geographic location, language, religion, heritage, or customs. Race and ethnicity are sometimes used interchangeably. They can overlap, such as a person who identifies as Chinese-American and practices both the customs of their Chinese ancestors and also American traditions—celebrating both the Chinese New Year and the American New Year, for example. The modern idea of race highlights a person's social and cultural origins rather than their biology. Ethnicity and race are fluid concepts.

However, bias *against* human populations based on race, religion, or ethnicity is blatant discrimination.

Regardless of religion, ethnicity, or culture, humans all belong to the same species. People may look different from each other, but we are all members of the human race.

MODERN ANTI-SEMITISM

Modern anti-Semitism draws its roots from the notorious publication *Protocols of the Elders of Zion* (often known as *Protocols*). Although the exact origin of the anti-Semitic literature is unknown, it was first published in Russian in 1905 as an appendix to *The Great in the Small: The Coming of the Anti-Christ and the Rule of Satan on Earth* by Russian writer Sergei Nilus. A complete work of fiction, *Protocols* claimed to be notes taken from a secret meeting with Jewish leaders. Its twenty-four chapters portray Jews as conspirators with covert plans to take over the world by controlling the media and economy and by igniting religious contention. The fabricated publication motivated worldwide anti-Semitism.

During the late nineteenth century and early twentieth century, Russian Jews were victims of three savage periods of pogroms. The Russian word *pogrom* describes the destruction, looting of property, rape, and murder of Jews between 1821 and 1921 in the Russian Empire and other countries, including Ukraine. The periods of savage killings each spanned several years, in waves of bloody desecration. During the civil war following the Russian Revolution in 1917, Red Army soldiers, Ukrainian nationalists, and Polish officials all contributed to pogrom violence that killed tens of thousands of Jews.

The hate and violence continued. The malicious lies of *Protocols* spread like wildfire. By 1920, the title had been translated and published in Russia, Poland, France, England, Japan, and the United States, as well as other European countries and throughout South America. Henry Ford, Amer-

This photo from 1881 shows members of the Jewish community examining Torah scrolls (sacred texts) that were damaged during one of the pogroms that swept through Russia.

ican industrialist and founder of the Ford Motor Company, also devoured the anti-Semitic hate. He owned a newspaper that ran an article series based off the *Protocols*, titled *The International Jew*. Although Ford later publicly apologized for his anti-Semitic rants, the articles were translated into

BLURRED LINES

Criticism of a government is normal. Citizens analyze and critique policies, holding officials accountable. The United States government is not immune to judgment, nor is the State of Israel. Disagreeing with and protesting government actions or policies is legitimate and socially acceptable.

However, criticism of the State of Israel sometimes crosses the line and morphs into outright anti-Semitism. But where is the line drawn? How does one tell if criticism sneaks over into discrimination? Israel's former minister for Jerusalem and Diaspora Affairs, Natan Sharansky, offers a quick test called the 3-Ds. If criticism demonizes, delegitimizes, or holds a double standard, it may be considered discrimination. Using anti-Semitic symbols to characterize Israel or Israelis, such as comparing Israelis to Nazi and Hitler, demonizes Jews. Denying the legitimacy of the Jewish state delegitimizes the Jewish right to exist. If Jews are measured by a different yardstick or selectively criticized, it is a double standard. You can identify and expose masked anti-Semitism with this quick test.

sixteen different languages and even caught the praise of Adolf Hitler.

As a German chancellor, Adolf Hitler was introduced to *Protocols* while he was constructing his worldview. Hitler developed an ideology founded in hate toward Jews, whom he viewed as a race of people. The anti-Semitic publication became an important tool in Nazi propaganda and was often used in schools to indoctrinate students. The Nazi party published twenty-three editions of *Protocols*. Hitler believed the extermination of the Jewish race, along with the disable, gay and lesbian, and Afro-German people, was needed in order to preserve Nazi survival. It was more than discrimination; the hate became state policy. During the Holocaust, six million Jewish men, women, and children were persecuted and murdered by the Nazi regime and other collaborators.

CONTEMPORARY HATE

Unfortunately, the *Protocols* are still prevalent today, despite the fact that they have been proven to be complete fiction and are intended to incite hatred of Jews and Israel. Hate groups in the United States and Europe circulate the *Protocols* as evidence that Jews are planning to take over the entire world. Some Arab and Islamic school textbooks teach the *Protocols'* lies as facts, and political propaganda and cartoons often include material from the publication. American and European neo-Nazi groups claim the Holocaust never happened. Extreme anti-Semitic ideologies still assert that Jews killed Jesus, despite religious leaders correcting the myth. In 1965, the Catholic Church stated that

Jesus' death "cannot be charged against all Jews, without distinction, then alive, nor against the Jews of today."

According to the Anti-Defamation League (ADL), an organization fighting anti-Semitism and all forms of bigotry, the number of violent anti-Semitic assaults rose 3 percent in 2015. Anti-Semitic incidents on American college campuses nearly doubled in that same year. However, not all crimes of abuse and discrimination are even reported. It is important to arm oneself with the tools to recognize, safely confront, and report anti-Semitism.

CHAPTER THREE

RECOGNIZING CONTEMPORARY ANTI-SEMITISM

T wo friends head to the coffee shop to grab a smoothie. Each orders and pays. One throws his leftover change, just a few pennies, into the tip jar. His friend remarks that he's being a bit *Jewy* with his tip, and throws in a dollar bill. Sometimes it can be difficult to properly identify anti-Semitism. Discrimination can be disguised as a demeaning joke, or it can be straightforward bullying. It also can materialize in several places. In order to call it out and stop it, one must first be able to spot it.

CROSSING THE LINE

All too often, the only anti-Semitism that the public hears about are violent incidents. The news may only report salacious and extreme hate crimes. Although these events are worthy of media coverage, slurs, bullying, and the use of hate symbols need attention, too. It is important to recognize all forms of discrimination, even those that are subtle. Anti-Semitic behavior in any form should not be considered normal or left unchecked. It can only foster a climate of hate tolerance.

"Harassment" or "bullying" is "unwelcomed intimidation that creates a hostile environment." Victims of harassment are targeted based on identifiers, such as race, ethnicity, and religion. It can occur in various forms, including verbal or physical bullying or using hate symbols. Hate speech or verbal bullying can be anti-Semitic. "Hate speech" is defined as "speech intended to degrade or disparage a person or group of people based on race, gender identity, sexual orientation, religion, or any other classification." This type of speech is not protected under the First Amendment. Verbal bullying can quickly escalate into bodily harm. Threats or stalking can erupt into physical violence, such as cornering a student in a secluded hallway or throwing pennies or stones at a victim.

Several friends and family attend the funeral of eighteen-year-old Eliyahu Asheri, who was kidnapped and murdered in an act of anti-Semitic terrorism in West Bank, Jerusalem.

In 2015 at a Denver, Colorado, high school, two high school students bullied a Jewish student wearing a kippha (a traditional Hebraic skullcap). They called him Jewboy and other anti-Semitic slurs. He ignored the hateful words, but they continued to harass him. Finally, the bullies threw a large rock, hitting the Jewish student on the back. Physical bullying should not be taken lightly. It is not "just fooling around" or "boys being boys." When not recognized and reported, this type of anti-Semitic bullying can only get worse.

Symbols are a quick and powerful way to communicate. Anti-Semitic symbols can be found just about anywhere, especially places where members of the Jewish community are likely to see them, such as the walls of a synagogue or in a school bathroom. Hate symbols are used as a form of harassment and intimidation. They are also a way to identify others who share the same anti-Semitic ideology, such as a swastika tattoo or a blood-drop cross t-shirt.

"Hate crimes" are defined as "violent incidents toward a person, or damage to property, based on identifiers, such as sexual orientation, disability, or religion." In the case of anti-Semitism, this would include swastika graffiti or desecration of Jewish graves. If a student randomly smashes a car window without regard to the car's owner, it is an act of criminal mischief. But if the student selects a vehicle because he has personal bias against Jews and the car's owner is Jewish, it is considered a hate crime subject to criminal prosecution.

HATE MAP

Some people achieve a sense of comfort when surrounded by people similar to them. They feel uncomfortable when confronted with an appearance or a culture different from theirs. These people can either choose to accept the richness of diversity in the world, or they can choose to reject others who are different from them. Jews have faced this rejection for the last

2,000 years, and the discrimination can still be found all over the world.

Anti-Semitism can happen in social settings, online, and even among the Jewish community. In a social setting, deliberately excluding someone from an event or embarrassing or humiliating him or her in front of a group are all forms of social discrimination and bullying. On November 29, 2016, at Ryerson University in Toronto, Canada, hundreds of students walked out in protest during a vote to implement a Holocaust Education Week on campus. Anti-Semitic students snickered

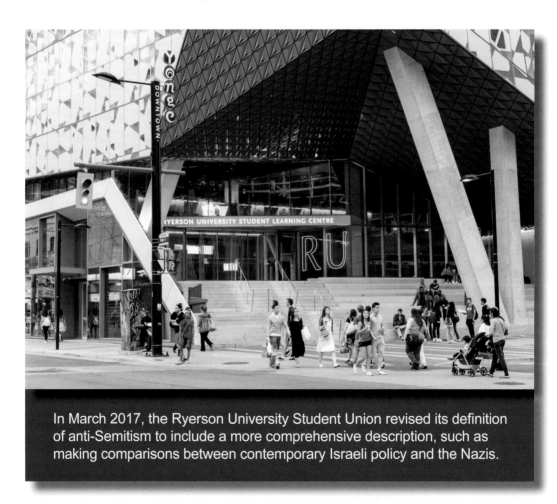

In March 2017, the Ryerson University Student Union revised its definition of anti-Semitism to include a more comprehensive description, such as making comparisons between contemporary Israeli policy and the Nazis.

and jeered when sponsors presented the idea to combat discrimination on campus. And when it came time to vote on the Holocaust Education Week, the anti-Semitic students stood up and left—essentially sabotaging the vote.

Instead of verbally assaulting a victim, cyberbullying happens online. When anti-Semitism happens online, the influence is widespread. More people see the attack, and the words never really go away. When bullied in a hallway, the victim can walk away; but how does one walk away from cyberbullying? Cyberbullying can take the form of threatening emails or text messages. Some cyberbullies steal passwords to other people's online accounts and send out messages using the stolen identities. Cyberbullying includes spreading hateful comments about Jews on blogs, social media platforms, and chat rooms. In Albany, New York, a Jewish high school was a target of cyberbullying. The school's website was hacked, and its homepage was replaced with threatening anti-Israel messaging and a Palestinian flag.

Anti-Semitism can even occur inside a Jewish community. A person may hear anti-Semitic jokes from other Jewish friends. This does not make the discrimination okay. The offender may justify the joke by claiming that it's not really anti-Semitic behavior because they themselves are Jewish. However, this kind of belief lends itself to accepting all forms of bigoted behavior.

AVENUES OF HATE

In the modern world, tools used to spread anti-Semitism are varied and accessible. Anti-Semitic messages and

I DIDN'T MEAN IT THAT WAY

Blatant or overt anti-Semitic discrimination, such as painting swastikas on synagogue walls or spreading rumors about Jewish people using human blood in baking recipes, is easier to pick out. Subtle discrimination is harder to distinguish and is often overlooked and ignored. Humor can be used as a subtle form of anti-Semitism. The offender may say she was just kidding or that it was meaningless. But if the joke doesn't mean anything, what is it trying to communicate? Jewish students may wonder if they are being too sensitive and believe a response might be an overreaction. Jokes using anti-Semitic myths or that belittle the horrific genocide of the Holocaust are not normal, even if it is commonly done or people don't often object.

Because subtle discrimination can be difficult to spot, it has more potential to manifest. A manager tells a Jewish employee that he is not ready to work the cash register, despite his proven skill with handling cash; the employee may wonder if he is being kept from interacting with customers (and money) because he needs more training or because he wears a kippah, but he would find this hard to prove without causing a confrontation. If the manager is, in fact, uncomfortable with his employee's display of the Jewish faith, then his anti-Semitic behavior goes unchecked.

images can quickly spread online through social media, blogs, or video-sharing websites. People with anti-Semitic views may spend time online trolling for places and people to target their hate, such as the comment section on blogs

The World Jewish Congress reported that more than 382,000 anti-Semitic posts were shared to social media platforms in 2016. That is an average of one hate post every eighty-three seconds.

or the Twitter pages of Jewish public figures. They use their hateful words to garner media attention. Any publicity is good publicity, and it helps to spread their message.

At its worst, hate can even step from the virtual world into reality. The Alt Right group started as an online movement but has pushed into real-world activity. The hate group organizes in-person meetings and conferences to rally and network with members while planning actions in cities across the United States. Many streams of anti-Semitic hate target youths for recruitment to expand their movement. It is important to be vigilant and to recognize anti-Semitism, regardless of where it comes from or what form it takes.

CHAPTER FOUR

HEAR SOMETHING, SAY SOMETHING

Former national director of the ADL Abraham Foxman often highlighted that the gas chambers of Auschwitz did not start with bricks but with words. His point is a potent reminder that when verbal forms of anti-Semitism, such as slurs, jokes, stereotypes, or myths, are not confronted, these vile words can evolve into serious acts of violence. To break the cycle of hate, one must take steps to stop anti-Semitic abuse. Confronting discrimination involves learning effective response strategies and committing to standing up for the human right of a life free from hate.

CALL OUT AND CONFRONT

People can be involved in an incident of discrimination in at least one of four ways: as the bully, the victim, the bystander, or the upstander. The *bully* singles out and targets a Jewish student. The *victim* is the object of the abuse. The *bystander* witnesses the discrimination but chooses to do nothing about it, neither confronting nor reporting the incident. The *upstander* also witnesses the incident but chooses to safely confront the bully

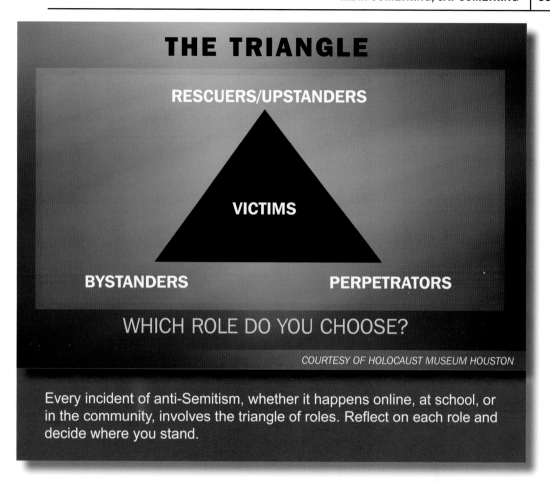

THE TRIANGLE

RESCUERS/UPSTANDERS

VICTIMS

BYSTANDERS   PERPETRATORS

WHICH ROLE DO YOU CHOOSE?

COURTESY OF HOLOCAUST MUSEUM HOUSTON

Every incident of anti-Semitism, whether it happens online, at school, or in the community, involves the triangle of roles. Reflect on each role and decide where you stand.

and support the victim. The upstander helps end the harassment and becomes part of the solution instead of adding to the problem.

When experiencing physical, verbal, or emotional discrimination, take the proper steps to respond and confront the bigoted behavior. First, ensure your safety. If needed, simply walk away. Do not try to fight or retaliate with bullying—this action may perpetuate the cycle of hateful behavior. If a bully has a weapon or threatens serious physical injury or hate-motivated violence, contact a school authority or the police. Personal safety is most important. However, if you feel safe to do so in the situation, consider saying something. Before you blurt anything out, you should first do an emotional check-in. If your emotions are raw, it may be best to wait until later to effectively respond. If your emotions are in check, tell the aggressor to stop in a firm but calm and collected manner. At this point, hopefully, the confrontation will help to defuse the situation. If not, walk away.

After the incident, talk to a trusted friend about what happened. Feelings of shame or self-hated can occur after the abuse. Reach out to a social support group. Ask friends to buddy up when and where the bully or bullies tend to attack. There is power and safety in numbers. The most important step to take after witnessing or being the victim of anti-Semitic discrimination is to report it. Don't let the behavior go unchecked, even after confrontation.

HATEFUL CHATTER

Whether discrimination happens in a school hallway or on a social media website, there are ways to proactively and safely confront the behavior. Targets of cyberbullying should not respond directly to their attackers. Resist forwarding the incident to friends. It may be tempting to press delete, but it is important to save evidence. Take screen shots. Keep copies of text messages or emails. Record the dates, times, and a detailed description of what was said, who said it, and even who spread it. This evidence can be used when reporting the anti-Semitic incident. Defend against future cyberbullying opportunities by changing screen names, blocking the offender on social media sites, or securing new contact information,

IT WAS JUST A JOKE

Humor slides into harm with the delivery of anti-Semitic jokes. Friends who make an offensive joke may do so out of ignorance. They could be repeating slurs or stereotypes heard or learned without regard for or effort to understand the meaning of the hurtful remarks. This is a prime opportunity to respectfully call them out and educate. First, assess the situation. Reflect on what was said, and consider if it's an effective time to engage with the offender. If emotions are heightened, then it may be best to respond later during a one-on-one conversation. If the time is right, address the comment or joke. Ask the offender what he or she meant to communicate with the joke. Most importantly, engage in respectful dialogue. Help the person understand that the words hurt and only perpetuate stereotypes. Acknowledge that the joke may not have been intended to harm, but it did—and explain how.

The offender may repeat the anti-Semitic humor, but don't be afraid to remind them that their words are not acceptable. A person's sense of humor cannot be controlled or dictated, but a victim always has the right to call out discrimination when it happens, even when it's unintentional.

such as a new email address or cell phone number. Online hate speech that does not target a specific person still affects the Jewish community. Most sites, including Facebook or YouTube, allow users to flag aggressive or hate-based content. Speak out against hate speech by posting videos, articles, or op-eds that oppose negative ideology. Share and comment positively on content that promotes diversity.

Sometimes anti-Semitic behavior can happen in unlikely places, such as a classroom. Teachers and other school authorities are expected to protect and respect students of all backgrounds. But in some schools, this may not be the case. Teachers or staff may engage in anti-Semitic slurs or jokes. For example, in 2015, a Brussels high school teacher was investigated after telling a Jewish student that all Jews should be put on freight wagons. (During WWII, Nazis rounded up Belgian Jews and put them on these sorts of vehicles in order to send them to death camps in Poland.) If this happens, seek out the advice and help of a trusted adult. Anti-Semitic discrimination is never acceptable, whether it comes from a classmate, co-worker, or teacher.

WHAT NOT TO DO

Ignoring, excusing, or becoming immobilized by fear when witnessing anti-Semitism is exactly what not to do. As Jewish writer and Holocaust survivor Elie Wiesel once said, "What hurts the victim most is not the cruelty of the oppressor, but the silence of the bystander." Shift from being a bystander to an empowered upstander by proactively standing up against anti-Semitic behavior.

UNITED WE STAND

Growing up in Sweden's third largest city, Malmö, Siavosh Derakhti was seven years old when he first witnessed anti-Semitism. His two best friends were David, a Jew, and Juliano, a Roma. Derakhti is Muslim, which is a minority in Sweden—but Jews make up an even smaller percentage of the population. Muslim kids used to pick on David, calling him a dirty Jew. Derakhti defended David, telling the bullies to shut up and stop talking to his friend that way. He also became a target for the bullies. They labeled him a traitor because he was protecting a Jew.

Founder of Young People Against Anti-Semitism and Xenophobia Siavosh Derakhti attended the Micael Bindefeld Foundation in Memory of the Holocaust event in Stockholm, Sweden, in 2017.

At nineteen years old, Derakhti founded a group called Young Muslims Against Anti-Semitism that evolved into Young People Against Anti-Semitism and Xenophobia. He has led busloads of Swedish teenagers to Auschwitz and other concentration camps to

(continued on the next page)

(continued from the previous page)

remind them of the devastation of anti-Semitism and to inspire them to fight against hate. Despite his good work, Derakhti still faces discrimination from his own Muslim community. He has even received death threats. But he is dedicated to fighting the continued hate of Jews in Europe and elsewhere in the world. Derakhti received the 2013 Raoul Wallenberg Award for civic courage.

If you witness classmates being bullied or overhear an anti-Semitic joke, say something. Help the victim, even if the person is a stranger. If safety is an issue, help the victim to a safe place. Be available for support. Know your school's bullying policies, and get involved in organizing a campaign that recognizes allyships and upstanders. When new students enter the school, befriend and welcome them.

In 2007, two high school friends, David Shepherd and Travis Price, noticed a new student was being bullied after he wore a pink shirt to school. Shepherd and Price decided that they wanted to do something about it. They went out and purchased a bunch of pink t-shirts and distributed them to students. The hallways were flooded with pink. Since their simple but proactive move, February 22 is annually celebrated as Pink Shirt Day. The event promotes kindness and fights against bullying in schools.

Remaining silent is not an option, but a zero-tolerance policy may not always be the best prevention and intervention strategy. Zero-tolerance policies suspend the bully after one or more incidents. Although it is important to have consequences and not

A firefighter wears a pink shirt to celebrate Pink Shirt Day in Richmond, British Columbia, on February 22, 2015. The annual event highlights anti-bullying and raises awareness of discrimination in schools.

let behavior go unchecked, this policy can raise other issues. Threats of suspension or expulsion may prevent students from reporting the discrimination. Also, bullying can be a gateway to other types of problematic behavior, such as fighting or theft. These students need positive role models in their lives, such as teachers. Ditch the Label is an online anti-bullying nonprofit promoting an alternative solution. They propose getting rid of the labels "bully" and "victim" to bring the situation back to the root cause—a behavioral issue. The organization believes bullying is a behavior and not an identity. Ditch the Label supports those who have been targeted and works on prevention and recovery strategies with offenders.

CHAPTER FIVE

NO JUSTIFICATION FOR DISCRIMINATION

R eporting the incident is just as important as confronting discrimination. When anti-Semitism is reported, it helps institutions, such as schools or local governments, keep track of the abuse. Part of finding a solution to a problem is understanding when and where it happens. When anti-Semitic hate is not confronted or reported, it poses a threat to the democratic values of all people, especially other minorities who are also at risk of discrimination. Anti-Semitism is not a Jewish problem; it is an issue for all of society.

REPORT IT

The Bureau of Justice Statistics estimates that two-thirds of hate crimes are not reported. Some victims feel ashamed or worry that nothing will be done. But if a victim or witness does not report it, then who will? If hate goes unchecked, it can grow and fester. Exposing anti-Semitism will help law enforcement build prevention and response strategies. Plus, reporting can help resolve the incident and offer a sense of closure for victims, allowing them to move forward and help others in the future.

Identify the correct person or agency to contact based on where the incident occurred. If it happened on a school campus, find a trusted teacher or guidance counselor to whom you can report the discrimination. Check if your school is using one of several bully-reporting phone applications, such as STOPit or Save Our Students (SOS). These apps allow students to anonymously report the harassment and include evidence of the offense, such as photos or video. If you witness discrimination against a student you don't know, it is still important to contact an authority figure. Sometimes victims won't report an incident because they fear retribution or feel that they might be overreacting to

Austin Kevitch turned lemons into lemonade. He is the founder of Brighten, an anti-bullying application that allows users to anonymously send notes of kindness, such as a compliment, to others.

the abuse. Always report anti-Semitism to ensure that school authorities can keep an eye out for future incidents and contact the victim to offer support.

Cyberbullying and harassment often breach terms of service with social media sites and Internet service providers. When in doubt, check out terms and conditions for the site or learn how to block a user. If the discrimination persists, file complaints and report cyberbullying with social media websites, Internet service providers, or cell phone companies. They can investigate the evidence, find the offender, and terminate their accounts if they are violating the terms of service.

When reporting an act of vandalism in the community, file a report with local law enforcement. If you are witnessing an act of physical violence or someone is in immediate risk of harm, call 911. Similarly, if cyberbullying involves threats of violence or stalking, contact the police. Depending on state laws, the offense may be considered criminal behavior. Cyberhate is often linked to terrorist acts and violence against Jews. If cyberbullying involves students or teachers from your school, report the incident to school authorities. Often, online harassment is related to in-school bullying. In many states, schools are required to tackle cyberbullying as part of their anti-bullying policy.

Employees who feel they have faced or witnessed religious discrimination should first address the concerns with the offender. If they ignore the complaint, contact the company's human resources representative. Keep records of what happened, as well as others who witnessed the discrimination. An employee can also report an anti-Semitic incident with the Equal Employment Opportunity Commission. If you are worried about being punished for reporting, don't be—the law legally protects an employee or applicant for opposing, reporting, or participating in a legal investigation of discrimination.

All anti-Semitic incidents, regardless of where they happen, should be reported to organizations that work toward fighting discrimination and hate. The ADL is a nonprofit that works toward stopping defamation of Jewish people, as well as all forms of bigotry. They invite reports on anti-Semitism, racism, or other bigoted incidents. Other groups that also track hate are the Ephesus Initiative, Amnesty International, and the Southern Poverty Law Center.

The US Equal Employment Opportunity Commission enforces federal laws that make it illegal to discriminate against an employee or job applicant because of their religion.

EVIDENCE OR CORROBORATING MATERIAL

When reporting an act of discrimination, strong supporting evidence can empower the report. Collect as much evidence as possible, including photos of vandalism, screenshots of online abuse, and saved text of instant messages and emails. Keep track of dates, who was involved, and any voicemail messages. Collecting indirect and direct evidence will help the authorities dissect how to approach the incident.

Follow up with school officials or law enforcement after reporting an incident, especially if the anti-Semitism continues. Ask how they plan to prevent abuse in the future. Make sure action is taken and the evidence doesn't get lost or ignored. An upstate New York school district ignored several repeated anti-Semitic acts that plagued the hallways for years. Jewish students were bullied with Nazi salutes and anti-Semitic slurs. One student was held down while bullies tried to shove coins down his throat and called him a "dirty Jew." School officials responded but failed to take serious action. The abuse continued until a lawsuit was finally filed against the school district.

KNOW YOUR RIGHTS

After reporting, victims and their allies may discover laws and policies that protect their human rights. The Civil

An anti-bullying sign is proudly displayed in the hallway of Adams Elementary School in Janesville, Wisconsin. Learn your school's anti-bullying policy and share it with others.

Rights Act of 1964 prohibits discrimination based on religion in public schools, including colleges and universities. Most teachers and school officials understand the importance of providing a safe learning environment free from discrimination and hate. State and federal laws also protect students from cyberbullying. Public schools in some states are required by law to develop polices prohibiting cyberharassment. Check with your school regarding polices or consult the student handbook. If school officials do not follow up with action or do not adequately address the anti-Semitic incident, contact the State Department of Education or the Office for Civil Rights with the US Department of Education.

Title VII of the Civil Rights Act of 1964 prohibits employers from discriminating against an employee based on religion or for wearing religious garb, such as a yarmulke. If an employer asks a Jewish employee not to wear a kippah when interacting with customers, it would be considered discrimination and in violation of the Civil Rights Act. In addition, the law requires employers to offer reasonable accommodation for the religious beliefs and practices of the employee. Exceptions to dress codes or flexible scheduling are examples of accommodation.

Hate crime laws enforce tougher punishments on criminals who target their victims based on race, ethnicity, sexual orientation, gender, gender identity, disability, or religion. The laws state that it is a crime to use force or threats when a person is participating in federally protected activities, such as public education, employment, or any public activity.

10 GREAT QUESTIONS
TO ASK A SCHOOL OFFICIAL WHEN REPORTING ANTI-SEMITISM

1. What is the process for reporting an anti-Semitic incident?

2. Is there a team of teachers that allies itself with victims of discrimination?

3. Will the victim's identity be confidential? If not, do you have policies that address or protect students from retribution?

4. What are the school's bullying policies?

5. What is the school's policy on hate crimes?

6. How is bullying addressed in the hallways or in classrooms?

7. How will the school follow up with both the victim and the offender?

8. Do school officials report the anti-Semitic hate crimes with an organization such as the ADL?

9. How is the Holocaust taught, and are there ways to combat anti-Semitism through the lesson plan?

10. Can the school organize an educational event that focuses on religious inclusiveness and tolerance?

CHAPTER SIX

STAY CALM AND CARRY ON

Although anti-Semitism is on the rise around the world, Jewish and non-Jewish communities are joining the fight against hate. Several resources are available for those who suffer the abuse or those who wish to combat it. Remain steadfast and celebrate victories. Investigate opportunities to educate communities and increase awareness. It's important to remember that you are not alone in this fight.

IT'S NOT YOU, IT'S THEM

Dealing with anti-Semitism is a difficult process and can cause a great deal of suffering. Experiencing and confronting discrimination can take a toll on the mind and body. Victims may experience stress, anxiety, and depression. The effects of anti-Semitism reach beyond real-time incidents; other Jewish people in the community may also begin to feel a heightened sense of fear, anticipating the next hate crime. Other minorities can feel a wave of dread. Even witnessing the overt hate can cause symptoms of stress.

Being bullied messes with one's head. Victims may begin to internalize the negativity and even start to believe the hateful words. It's important to find healthy ways to manage the strain. Resist the urge to ignore and squash the feelings. Find healthy ways to cope. If you are feeling weak from discrimination, zero in on your core values and strengths. Seek out support systems. Find others who have gone through discrimination as well. It can be comforting to know you're not alone and brain-

On February 1, 2017, members from the Washington Islamic Society of North America and the American Jewish Committee met with politicians to discuss ways to fight religious discrimination.

storm ways to heal from the experience. Friends and family can also validate the victim's reaction to anti-Semitism. Sometimes, it can be easy to doubt feelings and want to forget the whole thing. While it is important to move on, it's also essential to reflect on what happened and to prevent future incidents. Don't dwell, but don't forget. If all else fails, seek professional help. There is no shame in reaching out; it's the smart thing to do.

EDUCATE, DON'T DISCRIMINATE

School is a place that should be free from hate. Every student, regardless of religion, has the right to a supportive and safe school environment. There are several opportunities to get the whole school involved in the fight against discrimination. Arrange for an assembly that addresses anti-Semitism from varying viewpoints. Invite a Holocaust survivor or someone whose family was affected by the Holocaust to speak at the event. Ask a representative from a local human rights organization to talk about ways to recognize and confront

I'VE GOT YOUR BACK

There are many ways to be a good ally and stand up against anti-Semitism. Don't participate in the discrimination. This may seem obvious, but standing around watching without confronting or reporting is merely a passive way of participating in the abuse. Don't laugh when an anti-Semitic joke is told. If it feels safe, tell aggressors to stop. If the bully happens to be a friend, find a moment in private to tell them that their behavior is hurtful, not only for the victim but also for you.

Support targets of discrimination, whether they are your best friends or complete strangers. Victims often feel isolated in the abuse, but a friendly offer to stand by them can be huge. Ask if they're alright and offer to walk with them or seek assistance. If you witness cyberbullying, step in and say something, or report the incident to the proper authority. Be an ally before and after an incident. Broaden your current circle of friends, and get to know people instead of judging them.

anti-Semitic acts. Summon those who are willing to share their personal stories of discrimination and how they handled the situation.

Ask teachers and library staff to organize a screening of a movie or video series that deals with anti-Semitism. Encourage the school librarian to create a display of both historic and contemporary examples of anti-Semitism, including newspapers, political cartoons, music, or films. How are teachers incorporating anti-Semitism into their lessons about the Holocaust? Identify opportunities in the current curriculum to address discrimination. A fun way to educate is to incorporate a multi-faith calendar. The ADL has put together a comprehensive calendar of

Holocaust survivor Nesse Godin spoke with students at Eastern Middle School in Silver Spring, Maryland. Here, the eighty-four-year-old survivor displays symbols that Jews and other minorities were forced to wear.

different religious observances in hopes of developing respect and education among different religious, ethnic, and cultural groups. It can be a great resource to use when planning school activities.

HATE-FREE ZONE

Anti-Semitic acts happen all over the world, but there are ways to fight back locally. Organize a community-wide fundraiser to raise money for victims or areas where anti-Semitic acts have taken place. In February 2017, a historically Jewish cemetery in St. Louis, Missouri, was badly desecrated when more than 170 headstones were overturned and damaged. The hate crime came on the heels of other anti-Semitic incidents in the area, including eleven bomb threats against Jewish Community Centers. The public fought back. Two Muslim activists, Linda Sarsour and Tarek El-Messidi, launched a crowdfunding campaign to fund the repairs of the damaged cemetery. They set out to raise $20,000 and met that goal in only three hours. By day three of the campaign, over 1,500 donors gave

On February 22, 2017, more than three hundred volunteers helped clean up the anti-Semitic vandalism at Chesed Shel Emeth Jewish Cemetery in University City, Missouri. Nabiha Quadri and Gwyn Thorpe work together during the cleanup.

more than $100,000. They plan to use all the funds to repair the Missouri cemetery and other vandalized Jewish graveyards around the country.

Organize an interfaith retreat that invites religious leaders from different places of worship, and Invite the public to learn about anti-Semitism and other forms of religious discrimination. Or start a small group at your house of worship, and brainstorm ways to become allies with other persecuted groups.

RISING ABOVE

Dr. Martin Luther King Jr. wrote in *Strength to Love*: "Returning hate for hate multiplies hate, adding deeper darkness to a night already devoid of stars. Hate cannot drive out hate; only love can do that." Be a role model for younger students. If you notice children participating any form of bullying, step in and say something. Point out that discrimination is hurtful and mean. Inform them that differences are not scary or something to poke fun at, but instead are an opportunity to learn about a new culture and perhaps make a new friend. Every day is an occasion to stand up to discrimination. Remember that slurs, offensive jokes, cyber harassment, and other forms of bullying are not normal behavior and should not be tolerated. Every human deserves a life free from hate. Oppression hurts us all. Hate and intolerance often stem from ignorance and fear. Create opportunities for dialogue and education. Practice compassion, and believe that some people can change. To achieve justice for all oppressed groups, we must fight any and all forms of bias, including anti-Semitism. We can and must rise above the hate.

GLOSSARY

anti-Semitism Discrimination against Jews and the Jewish religious community.

anti-Zionism Rejection of the right for Jews to have their own national homeland.

bigotry Prejudice against opinions or beliefs different from one's own.

bullying Unsolicited aggressive behavior toward another person, such as verbal or physical abuse.

bystander A person who witnesses discrimination but chooses to do nothing about it, such as confronting or reporting the incident.

cyberbullying Harassment using online communication, such as social media, text messages, or emails.

defamation Untrue speech or writing used to attack a person's reputation.

discrimination Unjust or unequal treatment of a person based on specific characteristics, such as race, religion, or sex.

ethnicity A person's identity within a group of people based on shared culture, language, and religion.

harassment Unwanted repetitive aggression or intimidation toward a person, such as threats or stalking.

hate crime A criminal act toward a person based on perceived race, religion, ethnicity, national origin, gender, or sexual orientation.

hate speech Communication intended to degrade or disparage a person or group of people based on a classification, such as race, gender identity, or religion.

hate symbols A visual form of harassment and intimidation.

oppression Unjust and cruel control or treatment of a person or group of people.

prejudice A preconceived negative belief without prior proof or knowledge.

race A group of people who share a common cultural origin or physical traits, such as skin color or eye shape.

racism Discrimination based on perceived race.

retribution An act of vengeance, or punishing someone for their actions.

stereotype An oversimplified generalization about a person or group of people.

upstander A person who witnesses discrimination and chooses to safely confront the incident.

Zionism A movement for the return of Jewish people to the Holy Land of Israel.

FOR MORE INFORMATION

American-Israeli Cooperative Enterprise (AICE)
2810 Blaine Drive
Chevy Chase, MD 20815
(301) 565-3918
Website: http://www.jewishvirtuallibrary.org
Facebook: @JewishVirtualLibrary
Twitter: @JewishVLibrary
The AICE is a nonprofit and nonpartisan organization
   dedicated to building a better alliance between the
   US and Israel. Their Jewish Virtual Library is a com-
   prehensive online resource of Jewish culture, politics,
   and history.

American Jewish Committee (AJC)
165 East 56th Street
New York, 10022
(212) 751-4000
Website: http://www.ajc.org
Facebook: @AJCGlobal
Twitter: @AJCGlobal
AJC is an international organization that advocates for
   the civil and democratic rights of Jewish people and
   Israel.

Anti-Defamation League (ADL)
605 3rd Avenue
New York, NY 10158
(212) 885-7700
Website: http://www.adl.org
Facebook: @anti.defamation.league
Twitter: @ADL_National

The ADL is a nonprofit dedicated to fighting anti-Semitism and all forms of discrimination. They aim to protect the civil rights of all people.

B'nai Brith Canada
15 Hove Street
Toronto, ON M3H 4Y8
Canada
(416) 633-6224
Website: http://www.bnaibrith.ca
Facebook: @bnaibrithcanada
Twitter: @bnaibrithcanada
Instagram: @bnaibrithcanada
B'nai Brith Canada is dedicated to combating anti-Semitism and protecting the human rights of Jews since 1875.

Canadian Civil Liberties Association (CCLA)
90 Eglinton Avenue E Suite 900
Toronto, ON M4P 2Y3
Canada
(416) 363-0321
Website: https://ccla.org
Facebook: @cancivlib
Twitter: @cancivlib
The Canadian Civil Liberties Association is a national civil liberties organization dedicated to fighting for the human rights of Canadian people.

Southern Poverty Law Center
400 Washington Avenue
Montgomery, AL 36104
(888) 414-7752

Website: https://www.splcenter.org
Facebook: @SPLCenter
Twitter: @splcenter
The Southern Poverty Law Center is dedicated to combating discrimination and seeking justice for marginalized members of society

WEBSITES

Because of the changing nature of Internet links, Rosen Publishing has developed an online list of websites related to the subject of this book. This site is updated regularly. Please use this link to access this list:

http://www.rosenlinks.com/SPKUP/Anti-Semitism

FOR FURTHER READING

Brezina, Corona. *Helping a Friend Who Is Being Bullied* (How Can I Help? Friends Helping Friends). New York, NY: Rosen Publishing, 2016.

Byers, Ann. *Anti-Semitism and the "Final Solution": The Holocaust Overview* (Remembering the Holocaust). New York, NY: Enslow Publishing, 2015.

Cohen, Robert Z. *Jewish Resistance Against the Holocaust* (A Documentary History of the Holocaust). New York, NY: Rosen Publishing, 2014.

Frank, Anne. *The Diary of a Young Girl*. New York, NY: Random House, 2011.

Grant, Michael. *Front Lines*. New York, NY: Harper Collins, 2016.

Hanson-Harding, Alexandra. *How to Beat Physical Bullying* (Beating Bullying). New York, NY: Rosen Publishing, 2013.

Lowery, Zoe. *The Nazi Regime and the Holocaust* (Bearing Witness: Genocide and Ethnic Cleansing in the Modern World). New York, NY: Rosen Publishing, 2017.

Mooney, Carla. *The Holocaust: Racism and Genocide in World War II* (Inquire and Investigate). White River Junction, VT: Nomad Press, 2017.

Sepahban, Lois. *Cyberbullying: 12 Things You Need to Know Tech Smarts*. Mankato, MN: 12-Story Library, 2016.

Silverman, Jean and Linda Bayer. *Elie Wiesel* (The Holocaust). New York, NY: Rosen Publishing, 2016.

Sonneborn, Liz. *How to Beat Verbal Bullying* (Beating Bullying). New York, NY: Rosen Publishing, 2013.

BIBLIOGRAPHY

Anti-Defamation League. "ADL Audit: Anti-Semitic Assaults Rise Dramatically Across the Country in 2015." Retrieved February 12, 2017. http://www.adl.org.

Anti-Defamation League. "Alt Right: A Primer about the New White Supremacy." Retrieved February 2, 2017. http://www.adl.org.

Anti-Defamation League. "Are You Ready to Be an Ally?" Spring 2012. http://www.adl.org/assets/pdf/education-outreach/Are-You-Ready-to-Be-an-Ally.pdf.

Anti-Defamation League. "Calendar of Observances." Retrieved February 17, 2017. http://www.adl.org/education-outreach/anti-bias-education/c/calendar-of-observances.

Anti-Defamation League. *Confronting Anti-Semitism Myths... Facts...*" Spring 2006. http://www.adl.org/assets/pdf/education-outreach/CAS-Myths-and-Facts.pdf.

Anti-Defamation League. "Global Anti-Semitism the New Threat: 90 Ways You Can Respond." Spring 2004. http://archive.adl.org/anti_semitism/new_threat/90ways.pdf.

Bureau of Justice Statistics. "Nearly Two-Thirds of Hate Crimes Went Unreported to Police in Recent Years." March 21, 2013. https://www.bjs.gov.

Echoes and Reflections. "Profile of Siavosh Derakhti." Retrieved February 13, 2017. http://echoesandreflections.org.

Federal Bureau of Investigations. "2015 Hate Crime Statistic Report." November 14, 2016. https://ucr.fbi.gov/hate-crime/2015.

Green, Jen. *Bullied by Groups* (Anti Bullying Basics). Chicago, IL: World Book Publishing, 2014.

Haaretz. "Belgian Teacher Tells Jewish Student: 'We Should Put You All on Freight Wagons'." February 10, 2015. http://www.haaretz.com/jewish/news/1.641706.

Jacobs, Thomas A. *Teen Cyberbullying Investigated: Where Do Your Rights End and Consequences Begin?* Golden Valley, MN: Free Spirit Publishing, 2010.

Jacobson, William A. "Anti-Israel Protest Disrupts Vote to Support Holocaust Education Week at Ryerson U." December 4, 2016. http://legalinsurrection.com.

Jewish Virtual Library. "Abraham 'Abe' Foxman." Retrieved February 17, 2017. http://www.jewishvirtuallibrary.org /abraham-quot-abe-quot-foxman.

King, Martin Luther, Jr. *Strength to Love*. Minneapolis, MN: Fortress Press, 2010.

Pope Paul VI. "Declaration on the Relation of the Church to Non-Christian Religions: Nostra Aetate." October 28, 1965. Retrieved February 10, 2017. http://www .vatican.va.

Raskin, Jamin B. *We the Students: Supreme Court Cases for and about Students*. Thousand Oaks, CA: Sage Publishing, 2014.

Senker, Cath. *Bullied by Friends* (Anti-Bullying Basics). Chicago, IL: World Book Publishing, 2014.

United States Holocaust Memorial Museum. "Protocols of the Elders of Zion." Retrieved February 10, 2017. https://www.ushmm.org/wlc/en/article.php ?ModuleId=10007058.

US Equal Employment Opportunity Commission. "Abercrombie & Fitch Settles Two Pending EEOC Religious Discrimination Suits." September 23, 2013. https://www.eeoc .gov/eeoc/newsroom/release/9-23-13c.cfm.

INDEX

A

Alternative Right/Alt Right, 13, 31
Amnesty International, 43
Anti-Defamation League (ADL),
    24, 32, 43, 51–52
anti-Semitism
    explanation of, 12–14
    history of, 16–17
    how to confront, 32–36
    how to recognize, 25–31
    modern-day/contemporary,
        20–24
    reporting, 40–43, 44
    tools/avenues of, 29–31
    ways to educate others,
        49–53
    what not to do, 36–39
anti-Zionism, 13–14
apps for reporting bullying, 41

C

Christian Identity, 13
Civil Rights Act of 1964, 44–45,
    46
cyberbullying, 29, 34, 42

D

Derakhti, Siavosh, 37–38
discrimination, explanation of,
    8–10
Ditch the Label, 39

E

El-Messidi, Tarek, 52
Ephesus Initiative, 43
ethnicity, explanation of, 18

F

Ford, Henry, 22
Foxman, Abraham, 32

H

hate crimes, definition and
    statistics, 8, 40
hate speech, 26, 36
hate symbols, 27
Hitler, Adolf, 22, 23
Holocaust, 23, 50

I

ideology, explanation of, 10

J

jokes/humor, 25, 29, 30, 32,
    35, 36, 38, 50, 53

K

Khan, Umme-Hani, 11–12
King, Martin Luther, Jr., 53

M

Marr, Wilhelm, 12

N

Nazis, 22, 23, 36

P

Pink Shirt Day, 38
Price, Travis, 38
Protocols of the Elders of Zion,
20–23

R

race, explanation of, 18
religious discrimination, explanation of, 11–12

S

Sarsour, Linda, 52
Sharansky, Natan, 22
Shepherd, David, 38
Southern Poverty Law Center, 43
subtle discrimination, 30

T

Traditional Youth Network, 13

W

Wiesel, Elie, 36

Y

Young People Against Anti-
Semitism and Xenophobia, 37

Z

zero-tolerance policies, 38–39
Zionism, 13–14

ABOUT THE AUTHOR

Kristina Lyn Heitkamp is a Montana-based writer, researcher, and science journalist. She earned a bachelor of arts in English from the University of Utah and a master of arts in environmental journalism from the University of Montana. She is the author of several children's articles and books, including *Gay-Straight Alliances: Networking with Other Teens and Allies*. Heitkamp is committed to fighting for the basic human rights of all people, regardless of race, religion, or gender identity.

PHOTO CREDITS